Fifth-Wave of the Feminist Movement Coochie Power 5.0 Era

21 Iconic Game-Changers for Feminism

Empowering Women to Plug into Power
In Celebration of the Most Pivotal Step in the
Movement

Marie-Antoinette Tichler

ISBN 978-0-9850263-7-0

Acknowledgements

A special thanks to the women who've poured their love & wisdom into me.
Julia Daniel, Edna McKinney, Florence Ray, Georgia Shields, Mary McKinney,
Nancy Sims (pictured above), Emma Daniel, Pauline Benson, Reaver Almond,
Earnestine Johnson, Marie Davis, Gloria Beasley, Mary Daily & Merel Mills.

A special special thanks for having my back through this project...
Steve Tichler, Tatianna Burrell, Karon Franklin, Donnie Daniel,
Kathy Patterson, Chantel Rachel & Shauntel Davis.

Much Love

About the Book

I wrote this book wanting to appeal to all women or anyone who knows a woman. This book is for you.

You don't have to read it all at once. Read it to draw strength from the past or pick it up when you need a dose of empowerment. Most of all, don't feel pressured to read it in order. If it touches you in any way, thank you for connecting to my hope for the future. While writing about the courage, tenacity, sacrifice, strength, resilience and creativity of the women in this book, of which I'm eternally grateful, it changed me. As I did the research and drafting, I could feel their presence so strongly around me it would give me chill-bumps and once even brought me to tears. I felt their hopes, wishes, and dreams pour over me. I was able to see them as women, regular women who did extraordinary things.

In less than five years we'll be celebrating the 100th Anniversary of Women's Right to Vote. The idea that the women of that time did so much, with less than one-third of what we have available to us in this current century is astonishing.

We are living in a LinkedIn, Facebook, IG, iCloud kind of world. We consider ourselves to be connected 24/7. You would think that among ladies, camaraderie, woman-support, sisterhood, would be at an all-time high, or the woman vs. woman rivalry would be considered a silly thing we used to do.

In fact, it seems to be just the opposite. I often hear things like, "Women are so bitchy, catty, and shady," "I hate working in an office full of women," "I hang out with dudes because women are back-stabbers and jealous," "I hate working for a Lady Boss," and, "I can't trust other women around my man."

What is up with that? Come on ladies! We can to do better and we will do better.

Writing this book heightened my gratefulness for the beautiful female relationships I've been so fortunate to have over my lifetime. I have female mentors, bosses, soldiers, entrepreneurs, CEOs, family and friends that have made a difference in my life. It's because of the same relationships that I have hope for other women to have the same.

My sincere hope is all women will experience the love of sisterhood, camaraderie, and woman-support. These questions sparked from my hope: how can we better honor the sacrifice of our women pioneers? How can the broken bridges be mended? How can women bond better? Can women master their Coochie Power? What will Fifth-Wave Fems accomplish? How can women plugging into their power change the world?

We all have a part in making this a better world. Our womanness has something to teach another woman. I need your womanness and you need my womanness to strengthen our womanhood. The journey of being a woman is not to be traveled alone. We need each other for a better tomorrow.

A Fifth-Wave Fem

Table of Contents

Preface

MY most formative years were deeply rooted in six decades of wisdom. I spent my youth with my paternal and maternal grandmothers and my great-grandmothers on both sides of my family. I attribute my most intricate learning to both Mrs. Edna McKinney, affectionately called Momma or Grandma interchangeably, and Mrs. Florence Ray whom everyone called Granny. During my formative pre-teen years, I spent my weekends, summers and holidays with these women and I learned much about how I wanted to be perceived as a woman.

Florence Ray

Granny's 60th birthday was the day after I was born. She was born April 8, 1911 in Georgia and I, of course, was born on April 7, 1971. This created a special bond between her and me. She was an impressive woman, standing slightly over six feet tall, actively faithful at church and beautiful in spirit and mind. Granny was a domestic worker in a home her children were not allowed in.

She married three times. One husband died. One husband left peacefully. And one husband was removed by an up-rising. Literally and physically forced to vacate by her children with sticks and rocks in hand. She owned her home in a time where that was rare, paid taxes for a school her children were not allowed to attend, did not drive, always wore an apron when she cooked, grew fruits and vegetables, canned fruit, dipped snuff and spit in a can, wore garter hose, made her own clothes, jams and homemade biscuits, and best of all, she kept her hair dyed a-hint-of blue. Granny was nice to everyone, always taking the high road. Extremely family oriented, Granny was known in the community as honest, reasonable, and fair. I didn't just love her as my Granny, I admired her approach to life, her kindness, honesty, and humor.

Edna McKinney

Grandma Edna was 61 years old when I was born. Born August 29, 1906 in Georgia. She was petite and appeared delicate. She was also actively faithful in the same church as Granny. Grandma Edna was widowed after fifty years of marriage. She was an entrepreneur, owned property and land, wore garter hose and muumuus, made homemade apple pies and biscuits, and still had a gentleman friend well into her 80's.

Grandma Edna bought her last car at 84 as an act of defiance. She was gentile and grew flowers as many women in the south of a certain class did at that time. She also had an eye for fashion and was a very stylish dresser. Even though her hair grew down to the middle of her back, she wore a Princess Leia bun similar to the one that Carrie Fisher wore in the movie "Star Wars."

Grandma Edna 'didn't take no shit.' She was guarded with her kindness and could spot an opportunist. You only had one time to even act like you were thinking about taking advantage of her and it was going down. Ms. Edna was known in the community as someone who was going to 'tell it like it is.' I loved her as my grandma and I admired her no nonsense style as a woman. I think she sensed my admiration and I was one of her favorites. She treated me special. Grandma Edna was kind, funny, and honest with me, and I appreciated her womanly ways then and now.

Marie-Antoinette

Granny and Grandma Edna shaped and formed me into a strong, confident, and free spirited woman. I've always been observant and inquisitive. Granny and Grandma Edna called it 'nosy.' Truth be told, they were just as 'nosy' and I learned from the best. I was rarely told to shut-up when I inquired about any subject, no matter the topic of inquiry.

They seemed to encourage my interest and both had different ways of listening. I would capture their full attention while vividly and excitedly filling them in on what I saw or heard. Today we call that giving the tea. Granny would sometimes have me perched by the stove, standing on an old wooden chair, stirring a pot of preserve jam as big as me with a wooden spoon. With it simmering on low, my mouth bubbled hot with news, or so I always thought.

Grandma Edna, on the other hand, had a crank washing machine and she would have me crank as I spilled my 'tea.' I have fond memories of being called a good helper; a skill I took pride in then and now. I would sometimes be standing on an old 2-foot tall wooden stool, directly facing the handle so I could use both hands to operate the machine, while my grandmother controlled feeding the clothes in the rollers. I'd be just "a-cranking and a-talking."

I literally talked for hours.

We enjoyed spending that time together and both my great-grandmothers allowed and encouraged my inquisitiveness and allowed me to express my opinion without demonizing, discouraging, discounting my views, judging me, or dismissing me.

Name of people in the photograph left to right. My father's side of the family. Willie Ed McKinney-Grandfather, Edna McKinney-Great-grandmother, Marie-Antoinette Tichler-me, Rodney Franklin-husband from 1991-1995, Ethel McFarland-Grandmother, Florence Ray-Great-grandmother

When I married at 20, it was my great-grandmothers, well into their 80's, that I turned to for advice. When I became a mother, my son began the fifth generation on my father's side of the family. It was both his-great-great grandmothers who prayed their blessings and wisdom over him. I was fortunate and proud that Granny and Grandma Edna were still there with their love and guidance. I had a quarter-century with these remarkable women and I strive every day to live in the shadow of the fine example they set for me.

Granny and Grandma Edna are the motivation for this book. I am writing this book for three major reasons. First, to pay homage to my Grandma Edna and Granny and all the Grandma Ednas and Grannies around the globe. Second, I want to honor their courage and determination to always be themselves, acknowledge their bravery and perseverance through the rough times. Most importantly, I want to honor their creativity, how they made having very little work, and moreover, the generosity of their spirit and the continuous outpouring of their wisdom and love.

I grew up with such phenomenal women in my life, who I'm pretty sure would never consider labeling themselves feminists, but who have become the strongest example of feminism for me and the muses for the future the feminist movement: Coochie Power. To these women, I say thank you. I am so grateful that they were my living examples; women who were plugged into their innate power and took the time to share and teach it to me.

The Centennial of the 1920's Women's Right to Vote

As we approach the 100th year anniversary of the 1920's Women's right to vote, the 19th Amendment, and combined with the projection that by 2020 there will be two billion female entrepreneurs, it's clear that this has been a tremendous leap forward.

My second reason for writing the book is that I want to start a conversation. Something huge is afoot. Women are on the precipice of tremendous opportunities for change in a revolutionary way.

My third reason for writing the book is that I want to be a part of the change and I want to empower woman to follow and join me in the revolution.

Some of my most important relationships today are ones that have been formed through transferring wisdom and sharing my life experiences. My growth and bond with women has evolved over time through many conversations about marriage, children, family, friendships as well as my military, corporate and entrepreneurial endeavors. I have a heightened awareness of the shared benefits derived from the communion of like-minded women and open dialogue about topics that are important to most of us. This heightened awareness has fueled my determination to share these benefits.

I want to honor the past and help spark the conversations for the future, through the "Fifth-Wave of Feminism and Coochie Power." I embark on this journey hoping to be a catalyst for change in the feminine mindset. I want to present different ideas, change points of view, transfer wisdom, and share ideas in a transparent, judgement-free zone. I feel this type of communal platform will change and inspire the thinking of women for generations to come.

I. Coochie Power 5.0?

Coochie Power 5.0 is designed to be an open, honest, and real form of feminist movement. Understanding where we are as women in the present and how we are supporting each other is important. Also, honoring where we came from and how we are celebrating where we're going.

This is a groundbreaking movement of encouraging women to honor the past, *Plug into Their Power*, and motivate them to reach back and share with other women, giving them the power to do the same. There will be no bra burning this go-around. Besides, bras are way too pretty and expensive for that now.

Still, I do hope to burn some new ways of thinking into an atmosphere of receptive women who want more and are working to achieve more. *Coochie Power 5.0* is about elevating minds to the next level of thinking. The Fifth Wave is a transformative experience, a manifesto of power, honoring the understanding of being an intricate piece of the end goal for enterprising women.

Today's women paying homage to the iconic women throughout history, past and present, who dared to make unapologetic, game-changing, and life-altering decisions; women who, against all odds, made a difference for all women and helped all people; women who fought for the right to vote, the right to make choices about their bodies, the right to own land, fair treatment at home and work, equal pay, and so much more.

What better way to celebrate a century of resilience, pride and courage? I cannot think of one. Can you?

What is Coochie Power?

Coochie Power is the power of a woman and her knowledge of self- worth combined, which endows her with the power to make informed choices and achieve her goals. It's about choice! The choice a woman has to do what she wants to do, when she wants to it, and how she wants it done.

Girl Power + World Power = Coochie Power

The celebration of the mystical, intangible powers that women possess like femininity, mothering, nurturing, healing, and strength as an active force in the global world. These powers do not just come from women who've given birth to children. Many of them are inbred in a woman's DNA and proliferated throughout their life experiences and some of these powers come from the soul, like the power of nurturing, which comes from the heart, and healing, which comes from the spirit of a woman. Finally, strength which comes from intuition and experience.

From the famous, spiritual, poignant, simple song tile of Bob Marley, "No Woman, No Cry," we all must use our unique powers to work together with a spirit of camaraderie, fairness, and respect to co-exist.

II. Can the "C" word and the "F" word co-exist?

The "F" word…Feminist. To some, it's just as grimy as the other "F" word or the "C" word "Coochie", or even grimier, the other "C" word, for that matter. And to the others, whose language include C's and F's, they are wondering what the big deal is.

Why the need to drag out the "F" or "C" word?

These words are the metaphor for the GREAT DIVIDE. The GREAT DIVIDE's two sides are:

•The level of tolerance the pioneers have for the recipients.

•The lack of homage the recipients show to the pioneers.

Would a Feminist say Coochie?

Feminist Era's	Generation Sub Names	Relational View	Era's Markers	Use the "C" or "F" word
Pre-Wave & First Wave *SUFFORAGE*	Prior-1920 1920-1960 GI Generation Silent Generation	Great-Grandmother	• Women's Suffrage • Educational Rights • Better Working Conditions	Not likely to use the "C" word Will use the "F" word
Second Wave *FEMINIST ACTIVITY*	1960-1990 Boom Generation Hippie Generation Joneses Generation MTV Generation Boomerang Generation	Grandmother	• Social Activism • Sexual Freedom • Political Gains	Not likely to use the "C" word More Likely to use the "F" word
Third Wave *Neo-FEMINISM*	1990-2005 Millennial Generation New Silent Generation	Mother	• Feminist Colorism • Cultural Differences • Sexuality	More likely to use the "C" word and the "F" word
Fourth Wave	2005-2020 PRE-Wired Generation	Daughter	• Spiritual • Global Socializing • Sexism	Highly likely to use the "C" word Not Likely to use the "F" word

First and second-wave feminists would have more of an issue with using the word Coochie. Third-wave feminists had less of a problem than the first and second-wave with using the word Coochie Fourth -wave Feminists do not have a problem saying the word Coochie. This HUGE disconnection is further discussed later.

Are you flying a Feminist flag and don't know it?

Do you believe that women:
• Should be the judge of what happen to their bodies?
• Can choose any career path they desire?
• Should make the same salary as their male counterparts?

If you answered yes any of the above questions, then you are a feminist, even if you're a male. Males can be feminist. It has absolutely nothing to do with being feminine. You are what would best be described as a feminist. The Feminist Movement is an evolving entity that transforms with what is required at that time.

The fact is, the original rules and laws governing our country were not written with women's best interest at heart. The feminists of the past made great strides in bringing women's best interests to the forefront, and feminists of the future are needed to continue the movement so that women's interests continue to be championed in our society.

Some common sentiments often expressed about women and feminism is, when will we ever be happy? We can vote. We can work. We can own our own home. We can make decisions about our bodies. We can marry whom we want. We can even become President of the United States. What is the big deal?

The big deal is that we still have things to work on and we wouldn't be able to do those things had it not been for women who worked together to make them happen. We need each other.

Feminism is not about being a victim, a man-hater, an elitist, an independent or dependent woman, or being butch, among other stereotypes.

A little Feminism lives within all of us. Even men. The struggle and sacrifice of feminism is evident in our everyday lives. Feminism is about being proud of womanhood, honoring the gifts of motherhood, and supporting others in the womanhood community.

The young ladies of the twenty-first century have been generationally primed for greatness by the voices and actions of women "Plugged into Their Power" displaying awesome, living examples, of Coochie Power.

They are ripe and ready to make a difference. They speak their minds, are culturally progressive, bravely intellectual, and focused go-getters. They read the important books of our time like "Lean In," "Red Queen," and "Daring Greatly;" sing along to innovative musical artists like Beyoncé, Taylor Swift, Rihanna, and JaNelle Mone; and are influenced by women like Amy Shumer, Laverne Cox, Mo'ne Davis, and The Kardashians. The young women of today publically share their ideals, opinions, and dreams. Everything about this carries the essence of our ancestors and deserves acknowledgement and celebration.

Five years from now we will be celebrating the 100th anniversary of the 19th Amendment, giving women the right to vote. Soon, American feminism will enter its fifth -wave, having experienced four waves, since its inception. The women who lead the movement in the early years were women just like the women of today, without any modern conveniences of course. They were regular women who, at some point, wanted better for their lives, and did something about it.

We have life as we know it today because they took action. We can draw from the bravery, strength, and tenacity of our pioneer feminists, and set out to accomplish anything we decide is worthy. By starting an open dialogue, we can learn from and honor the past. Covering the full range of life, including the un-had, uncomfortable, unmentionable conversations along with the most-had, familiar, light-hearted conversations.

III. Coochie Power in the Movement

The allure of the women in the Feminist Movement is their benevolence to what lies ahead, that exudes bravery and strength. Deciding that the status quo is no longer acceptable is rarely met with immediate applause. The willingness to not just want change, but take action, is remarkable and their accomplishments are astonishing. These are ordinary women who made extraordinary decisions; women who had big dreams, families, stress, and didn't have the Internet nor third-world problems.

Their decisions impact our voice, freedom, and body today. The most perfect example being the celebration of the 100th year anniversary of the 19th Amendment, our ability to do something that we may view as simple in today's times, vote. The Feminist Movement is a living breathing entity that has consistently evolved to meet the needs of the generation. These women are the wave-starters of the previous four feminist waves in the movement.

Pre-Wave

Margaret Brent was an early example of what was possible for American women. She was the first woman to own property and one of the first known suffragists in American history. In 1638, Margaret Brent, the first female lawyer in America, arrived in the Colony of Maryland. She was involved in over one-hundred court cases and was a major landowner.

Soujornor Truth radiated a relentless, resilient power. Her story of survival and dedication to women's rights and abolition can serve as a genesis of inner strength to draw from. A Dutch speaking African-American born into slavery in 1797as Isabelle "Belle" Baumfree, she was the first black woman to be honored with a bust in the U.S. Capitol.

By age 18 she had been bought and sold to three different slave masters, had being beaten and molested countless times, had two children, one died in childhood, and experienced the murder of her soulmate. After being forced to marry at age 20, the ebb and flow of her life brought her three children and a slave master's promise of freedom on the horizon. In 1826, Belle was close to 30 years old when her slave owner broke his promise. She was not set free. She escaped to freedom from her slave master with her infant daughter.

Two years later, in 1828, using the courts to recover her son, Belle became the first black woman to win such a case against a white man. It was not until the death of her son and a spiritual experience at age 46 that she changed her name to Sojourner Truth. She embraced feminism and really unleashed her relentless feministic power, setting her sights on ending suffering and bondage for all oppressed people with resilience and tenacity. Her best-known speech was delivered extemporaneously, in 1851. Sojourner's speech became widely known during the Civil War.

In 1870, she tried to secure land grants from the federal government to former slaves, a project she pursued for seven years without success. Ms. Truth even had a meeting with the President in the White House. In 1872, at age 75 she tried to vote in the presidential election, but was turned away at the polling place. She spoke about abolition, women's rights, prison reform, and capital punishment. She didn't allow her dream for change to be changed.

First-Wave

The First-Wave could be described as a quiet underground tsunami, the 1920's ushered in amazing tenacity, courageousness and strength. This consisted of organization, strategizing and mobilization, to get basic rights, win women's suffrage, female educational rights, better and fair working conditions. The first-wave of feminists focused very little on the subjects of abortion, birth control, and overall reproductive rights of women. First-wave feminists were a collection of women ranging from authors to militant activists.

Although the majority of them were more moderate and conservative than radical or revolutionary. They distinguished themselves as markers of change, forming the ideals, opinions, and objectives of feminists; emerging out of an environment of urban industrialism and liberal, socialist politics. The goal of this wave was to open up opportunity and equality for women, with a focus on suffrage, along with changing views about marriage.

Elizabeth Cady Stanton was an American suffragist, social activist, abolitionist, and leading figure of the early women's rights movement. Elizabeth initiated the first organized women's rights and women's suffrage movements in the United States.

Emma Goldman advocated passionately for the rights of women and is today heralded as a founder of anarcha-feminism, which challenges patriarchy as a hierarchy to be resisted alongside state power and class divisions.

Second-Wave

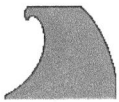

The second-wave of the feminist movement grew out of the first-wave until 1990. Second-wave feminism was a period of feminist activity that first began in the early 1960s in the United States and eventually spread throughout the western world and beyond, highlighting political issues, social issues, and cultural issues. The terms first-wave and second-wave were coined in March 1968 by **Marsha Lear**, writing in The New York Times Magazine.

This wave movement can arguably be recalled as the most tumultuous and plagued with internal conflict among women. Whereas the first-wave of feminism was generally propelled by middle class white women, the second-wave drew in women of color and developing nations seeking sisterhood and solidarity and claiming, "Women's struggle is class struggle." This era marks the genesis of division within the movement.

Beginning in the 1960s and continued into the early 1990s, this second-wave bombarded the scene in the context of the anti-Vietnam War and Civil Rights Movements and the growing self-consciousness of a variety of minority groups around the world. The voice of the oppressed was gaining volume and the voice of the second-wave was increasingly radical. In this phase, sexuality and reproductive rights were dominant issues, and much of the movement's energy was focused on passing the Equal Rights Amendment to the constitution in an attempt to guarantee social equality for all, regardless of race, gender, or sexual orientation.

In 1963, **Betty Friedan** published a book called The Feminine Mystique that identified "the problem that has no name." Amid all the demands to prepare breakfast, to drive their children to activities, and to entertain guests, Betty had the courage to ask, "Is this all there is? Is this really all a woman is capable of doing?"

In short, the problem was that many women did not like the traditional role society prescribed for them.

Gloria Steinem was launched as an icon of the modern feminist movement as the cofounder and editor of Ms. Magazine. Ms. Magazine was first published as a sample insert in New York magazine and 300,000 copies sold in 8 days. The first regular magazine issue was published in 1972 and became the major forum for feminist voices.

Third-Wave

The third-wave flowed through the 1990's to 2005, emerging with racial feminism, sexuality, and cultural issues. The third-wave of feminism began in the mid-1990s and was informed by post-colonial and post-modern thinking. In this phase, many constructs of society as a whole had been destabilized, such as marriage race and gender.

Many of the ideals of what make a woman had also been deconstructed, including the notions of universal womanhood, body, gender, and sexuality. A major aspect of third-wave feminism that bamboozled and annoyed the mothers of the earlier feminist movement was the reemergence by young feminists of the very lipstick clad, high heels wearing, and cleavage proudly exposed by low cut necklines, that the first two phases of the movement identified with male oppression.

This thinking is what single-handedly damaged the bridge in the movement. This thinking single-handedly damaged the movement and caused division among women that still exist today. Third- wave feminist were comfortable wearing bright red lipstick, sporting push-up bras, armed with generations of change and full of brains, this new era of women were bold and unapologetic. They stepped on the scene, on a campus or in the boardroom as strong and empowered, eschewing victimization and defining feminine beauty for themselves as subjects, not as objects of a sexist patriarchy.

Rebecca Walker coined the term third-wave feminism. She brought attention to the third-wave's focus on homosexuals and non-white women. Third-wave feminists have broadened their goals, focusing on ideas like homosexual theory and abolishing gender role expectations and stereotypes. Unlike the determined position of second-wave feminists about women in pornography, sex work, and prostitution, third-wave feminists were rather ambiguous, judgmental, and divided about these ideals.

Fourth-Wave

The fourth-wave, starting in the mid-2000's and projected to go into 2020, includes the climax of spiritual issues, blurred sexism, and rising to the evolution of social media. The Internet has emerged as an increasingly important space for feminist activists. The Internet has created connection, autonomy, and reach in which sexism or misogyny can be called out and challenged.

The current focus is on micropolitics and challenging sexism and misogyny insofar as they appear in everyday rhetoric, advertising, film, television and media, literature, and so on. The Internet has facilitated the creation of a global community of feminists who use the Internet both for discussion and activism.

Many commentators argue that the Internet itself has enabled a shift from third-wave to fourth-wave feminism around 2005. Advanced technology has advanced the evolution of the movement as well as widened the margin of disconnect, disrespect, and disgust between the wave eras. The birth of finger-wagging feminism resulted from individuals thinking and arguing things like you're not being a feminist the correct way; you're whining if you're a feminist; and feminism is a political issue.

The Internet has been a vehicle for the creation of a generation of breaking the glass-ceilings, gender ambiguity, celebrity-influenced ideals, and a call-out culture, in which sexism or misogyny can be called out and challenged. This culture of using social media sites as a medium has become known as Facebook feminism and is indicative of the continuing influence of the third-wave.

The mere existence of a fourth-wave has been doubted, without any grand demonstrations to mark the era, questioning that if more Internet usage by women can be enough to distinguish and delineate a new era. The number of women between 18 and 29 using digital spaces is rapidly increasing. The instantaneous nature of technology allows for a quick, reactive nature to feminist campaigns. This provides an opportunity for epic change on a massive scale, revolutionizing the feminist movements of the future.

IV. Breakdown of Coochie Power

My great-grandmother's generation would more than likely "feel some kind of way" about a few current norms that exist. I image that first through third-wavers would have an opinion about the "C" word and the mesmerizing effect of women like Nicki Minaj, Miley Cyrus, the Kardashians, or Jazz Jennings.

These are all women whose influence is possible because of the hopes and dreams of the pioneers who tirelessly worked for basic human rights and the freedom to choose. These women, like so many others to come, are the messengers of the times. So, in essence, every time we are able to experience the power of what a woman can do today we should celebrate.

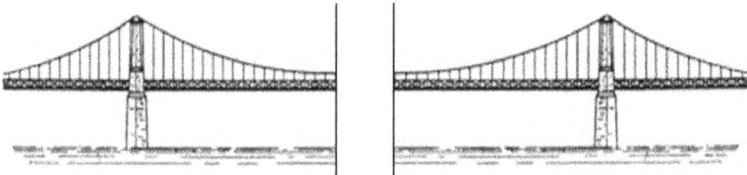

1. We need each other. Team work makes the dream work.
2. We can learn from one another. The past needs the future and the future needs the past.
3. We have the same goals: happiness, fairness, and freedom.

Breaking down the GAPS

The term "air dirty laundry" has been around since the 1800's, going from a literal term to a figurative action, like posting on Facebook. Silence has played a major role in American history, from a coping mechanism to a survival skill, when speaking out could mean certain death. It's been used as a fear tactic, a defensive tool when not saying anything was easier, and as o a moment of honor or show of support when paying homage to the past.

It is only in recent years that children have been viewed as having a voice, which is completely opposite of the old adage that children are meant to be seen and not heard. **Silence** is now an action reserved for occasions and no longer a way of life. We are in the Age of Transparency; being open, honest, real and sometimes raw. Making this transition, for some, can be a bit much to handle.

Learning, practicing, and implementing not to pre-judge, judge, or pass judgement is just as new a concept as airing dirty laundry. The age of technology has given us the opportunity to see into each other's souls, kitchens, houses, lives, and everything else. This has equally opened the door to old school damnation, shame and judgement.

Judgement in ways we've never been able to experience in the past, before the rise of mass communication technology like television, computers and mobile phones has become commonplace; judgements about how women are dressing, behaving, their lifestyle choices and religious beliefs. The effect of this way of being is that it causes physical separation and mental division, enabling more chances for us to band together.

Lastly, the passing down of wisdom to the next generation: **sharing**. The sharing of wisdom has definitely played a major role in human survival since the beginning of time. Sharing information was easier back then, whether over a bon-fire, a meal, or at church. Sharing, like silence, has evolved throughout time similarly as a survival skill to being a part of ceremony. Those historical reenactments, past stories, wise-tales, and folk-tales connected the family and community. In today's time, with overscheduled, over-worked, busy and bustling lives, getting together to share wisdom is not as high on the priority list.

21 MOST ICONIC GAME-CHANGING MOVES

What will the fifth-wave of the feminist movement bring? The ability to harness collective Coochie Power into action, openness, innovation, and inclusion will bring about unlimited possibilities. Paying homage to ordinary women, the women who dared to dream of a better life and did something about it, can serve as an excellent resource for strength, empowerment, and inspiration for women of today. Honoring where we've come from can assure that we move forward.

V. Coochie Power in Relationships

Rarely in American history has love been seen as the main reason for getting married. Marriage was considered too serious a matter to be based on such a fragile emotion. In fact, love and marriage were once widely regarded as incompatible with one another. Major shifts in relationship roles came swiftly after multiple wars, the emergence of the Feminist Movement, the Industrial Revolution, growth of a middle class, and access to contraception, reshaping relationship choices for women forever.

1

Used Relationship to Influence

ICONIC
GAME-CHANGER
FOR FEMINISM

Abigail Adams authentic selflessness exudes a steadfast stealth power. Her journey to change the world is easily believable to be divine intervention, beginning with her birth right, and ending as the only wife and mother of the President of the United States. Abigail was born 1774, into a deep political heritage and privileged social standing. She married her third cousin, whom she had known since they were children, at age 18.

In 10 years, Adams gave birth to six children. When her husband was elected President and the capital was moved to Washington, Abigail became the first lady to reside at the White House. Mrs. Adams took an active role in politics and policy, understanding that her ideals and opinions were not welcomed with joy and excitement. Hearing "No" or facing rejection or objections didn't crumble her spirit.

Over the course of her marriage, she and her husband created a large collection of correspondence between them. Mrs. Adams openly expressed her ideals, proposals, and persuasions about a variety of subjects. She was a strong advocate of women's rights, always encouraging her husband and other members of the Continental Congress to "remember the ladies" as they began the work of crafting the new American government. Abigail lovingly leveraged her relationship with both her husband and son for the benefit of citizen fairness, women's suffrage and rights, and other issues she believed in.

2

Wrote About Marital Rape

ICONIC
GAME-CHANGER
FOR FEMINISM

Lucy Stone was an independent woman whose expressions exuded bold, courageous powers. She was born in August, 1818, to a self-described life of opulence to an entrepreneur mother and financially controlling father. As a child, after experiencing her mother stealing her money back from her father, Lucy vowed to never depend on a man to take care of her. In addition, as a youth, she was deeply influenced by the biblical passage, "and thy desire shall be to thy husband, and he shall rule over thee." (Genesis 3:16)

Lucy decided to keep control over her own life by never marrying, obtaining the highest education she could, and earning her own money. Her first job as a teen was as a teacher. This taught her about the hurt of unequal pay and further charged her journey for fairness and change. Determined to obtain a higher education, she enrolled in seminary at the age of 21, and withdrew only a month later because of the seminary's intolerance to women's rights and anti-slavery.

Four years later, at age 25, and after changing schools the very next semester, Lucy traveled by train to the country's first college to admit both women and African Americans. This life-altering time segued into her creating life-long friendships, becoming the first female college graduate from Massachusetts, and accomplishing a career goal of becoming a public speaker by 28 years old. At age 32, while traveling in Indiana, she contracted typhoid and almost died.

After her recovery, Mrs. Stone re-entered the scene, unknowingly creating a viral new short shirt with pants "bloomers" style trend, which she abandoned later feeling like it distracted from her message. At age 35, after two years of courtship, she married in 1853, requiring a marital contract very similar to what we consider a pre-nuptial agreement today, Including stipulations like: she can choose when to have children, how many children to have, can have property in her name, she can will her property in death to whomever she wishes, keep her maiden name, keep her earnings from working, and she would pay her own expenses in the marriage.

A couple years later, Lucy wrote a letter expressing her stand on marital rape, making history by speaking out on a highly taboo subject. A few years after marriage she had two children, of which only one survived, a girl. By age 52, in 1870, she'd reversed her opinion about divorce, which caused major drama with other women in the newly forming movement.

This is why some critics would say, "Ms. Lucy doesn't get the appropriate credit to the Women's Suffrage movement she deserves."

At age 61, she was refused and turned away at the voting polls for trying to vote using her maiden name. Mrs. Stone continued to write articles about rape and crime against women in her later years, demonstrating her lifelong dedication to the movement.

3

Born Free Black Suffragette Voice

Naomi Bowman Talbert Anderson was an early example of how insight exudes the power of selflessness. She advocated for equal rights for all genders and races in the 1870s. She was one of three children born in 1843, a free black to free black parents of moderate means.

Her mother valued education and when she was unable to attend the all-white schools in town she hired private tutors. This early act of discrimination ignited a determination to break barriers and change things. By 12 years old, Naomi became the first black person to attend the all-white school in the same town, after impressing the white community with her poetry.

Her mother's death when she was 17, ended her dream and support to attend college. Her father thought that additional education for her was unnecessary. By 1868, when Naomi was 25 years old, she had gotten married, buried her only siblings, birthed two children, buried one, and moved a few times, ending up in a bustling, progressive city. This was where, within one year, she became a voice of her generation; a black suffragette speaking at the first Woman's Rights Convention in 1869.

Ms. Talbert was a literary pioneer, whose rare published works are an early example of public protest by a black woman. She wrote poetry and gave speeches high-lighting the experience of black women, enslaved by their inability to vote. Anderson had two more children before her husband became ill and died in 1877, when she was 34 years old. Shortly thereafter, she and her family moved again, where she met and remarried four years later. Naomi's voice of discomfort about the mistreatment of individuals because of their race, sex, or gender continued throughout her life. By 1892, Ms. Anderson worked alongside white suffragists, who praised her work, to campaign for one of the nation's first state woman suffrage referendums.

4

First Generation Feminist

ICONIC
GAME-CHANGER
FOR FEMINISM

Harriot Eaton Stanton Blatch was a woman whose fearless dedication to her mother's dream exuded graceful, powers of homage. Born in 1856 to comfortable privilege and social activism, Harriot inherited the cause, becoming the first daughter of pioneering women's rights. Her mother was an American writer, suffragist, and activist, and her father was a popular orator and writer who used these skills as a journalist, attorney, and politician.

She graduated college in 1878 with a mathematics degree at age 22 and traveled to Germany as a tutor for young girls. On a visit back home to the United States in 1881, two things happened that forever changed her life. Harriot met her soon to be English husband and worked on the women's suffrage movement with her mother and other iconic first-wave feminists. Her contribution was a major move of inclusion, though seen as controversial at the time, later it helped to reconcile the movement.

She got married at 26 and resided with her husband near London for 20 years, where she had two children. Only one survived. Mrs. Blatch returned to the United States at 46 years old wanting to reinvigorate the American women's suffrage movement, which had gone stagnant by 1902. She could organize a militant street protest and expertly work the backroom politics required. She organized and led the 1910 New York Suffrage parade at age 54. Five years later, her husband died in 1915, after being accidently electrocuted.

Harriot was instrumental in the passing of the Nineteenth Amendment in 1920, along with many other women's right's issues. In 1939 at age 83, she suffered a fractured hip and moved into a nursing home. Her memoir was published and she died the very next year.

5

Interracial Marriage
ICONIC
GAME-CHANGER
FOR FEMINISM

Andrea Perez was a woman who dared to love and exuded the courageous power intrinsic to love. Andrea was born to working class, Mexican immigrant parents. She was the next to oldest of five daughters, a devout Catholic, and a good student. Perez was able to secure an assembly job and began to date an African American man she met at work. He was smitten with her and jumped at the opportunity to become her on-The-Job-trainer, carpooling together.

After a year of dating, Andrea was saddened by him being drafted into the Vietnam War. She welcomed him home after a year in war, their courtship bloomed, and in 1947, after two years of dating, they decided to get married. Miss Perez along with her fiancé, decided to take a political stand against the 1850's law prohibiting whites to marry anyone of color, and applied for a marriage license as a white woman marrying a black.

When her license was refused, a family friend and attorney was ready to take the case. Because Andrea and her husband were devout Catholics, her attorney argued that the Catholic Church was willing to marry them, therefore this impeded on her religious freedoms.

Andrea made history on October 1, 1948, by winning the first case of the 20th century to overturn a state miscegenation law. Her publicized, groundbreaking accomplishment was not celebrated by all. Her parents did not attend her May 7th, 1949 wedding. She eventually reconciled with her mother and father after the birth of her daughter.

VI. Coochie Power in Business

In 2020 we'll be celebrating the 100th year anniversary of The Women's Suffrage Act. That same year it is projected that there will be two billion women entrepreneurs. Women, including those with children, are currently over fifty percent of the labor force and have started more new businesses at a faster rate than men. More women have climbed into the ranks of middle management while the small number of women at the very top has held its own. For the first time in the history of American business, women who work are being perceived as a partial solution to solving social and economic problems, rather than the cause of the problems.

6

Equal Rights Equal Pay

ICONIC
GAME-CHANGER
FOR FEMINISM

Alice Paul was a woman whose bold, relentless actions demonstrated how intelligence is power. Alice was born in 1885, a decedent of the Quaker tradition as well as being reared with the Quaker attitude toward service. As a youth, she would sometimes attend suffrage meetings with her mother. She was the only one of her siblings to graduate from college in 1905, at age 20.

Alice earned her Master's degree two years later, then traveled to England to continue her studies. During her time in London, she encountered militant founders familiar with her plight, who became lifelong friends. Working with these women, she found her true calling as a soldier in the battle to win equal rights for women.

Within two years of her arrival in England, Ms. Paul was arrested seven times, imprisoned three times, and participated in hunger strikes while in prison. She believed in physically putting herself on the line. Her final imprisonment, where she was injured by being forced-fed, proved to be a bit too much.

Alice returned home to the US in 1910 to recover and develop a plan to work on the suffrage movement. She knew she was positioned to bring greater attention and scrutiny to the woman's suffrage cause, and used this power to shake up the stagnant American suffrage movement. Ms. Paul continued her studies, earning a PhD., law degree, an LLM, and a doctorate by age 45.

In between earning her degrees, she organized the 1913 Woman's Suffrage Parade, which had over a half million attendees and ended with the National Guard involved. Alice was the original author of a proposed Equal Rights Amendment to the Constitution at 38 years old. After 1920, she spent a half century fighting to secure constitutional equality for women.

Later in life, Alice Paul played a major role in adding protection for women in the Civil Rights Act of 1964, despite the opposition of liberals who feared it would end protective labor laws for women. She continued fighting for equal rights until she suffered a debilitating stroke in 1974. She died at the age of 92.

7

Civil Rights in the Workplace

Mechelle Vinson had a daring ability to fight for her rights and proved that perseverance is power. Born in 1955 and growing up poor, Mechelle was determined to fight for vindication, winning the first Supreme Court case for Sexual Discrimination in the Workplace.

She was 19 years old when she met a bank branch manager who offered her what she thought was a career opportunity. Ms. Vinson jumped at the chance and quickly excelled with her boss as her mentor. In a short amount of time she earned various job promotions on the basis of merit. Six months later, things changed when Mechelle accepted her boss's invitation to dinner.

She was expected to *thank him* for what he'd done for her. Ms. Vinson resisted for as long as she could, but eventually gave in out of fear of losing her job. This led to repeated proposed sexual relations, including approximately forty or fifty occasions of intercourse, sexual interludes in his office and the bank vault, sexual relations during and after work, being fondled in front of employees; being followed into the women's restroom, the boss exposing himself to her and raping her on several occasions.

Mechelle was afraid to report the incidents or use the bank's complaint procedure out of fear. Around 22 years old Vinson began dating someone steadily, and her bosses' behavior stopped. Some months later, she took a leave of absence indefinitely. Two months after taking her leave, she was fired. Ms. Vinson filed a lawsuit against her old job for sexual harassment. At 31 years old, Mechelle made history, changed history, and was vindicated when the Supreme Court ruled in her favor.

VII. Coochie Power in Health

Prostitution in the United States is not illegal at the federal level. The regulation of prostitution in the United States is not among the enumerated powers of the federal government. Why is a women's womb even a topic of conversation at all? This may or may not be a great conversation starter, but anyway here is it.

Let's do some menstrual math. Most cycles last on average 5 days, about every 28 days, so in a lifetime (average 40 years) a woman has to deal with their menstrual cycle on average 62,500 hours. 62,500 hours of physical health maintenance, use of products, and coordination of whatever has to be done to get through. It's not a walk in the park, stroll on the beach, or prance in a meadow for women. It's simply part of a woman's life that we all have to deal with; no wearing white, childbirths, doctor appointments, mood swings, cramps, hot flashes, health issues…. The list goes on. Women get well over the 10,000 hours of practice needed to master the task of managing our bodies.

8

Women's Right to Birth Control

ICONIC
GAME-CHANGER
FOR FEMINISM

Margaret Louise Higgins Sanger was a daring woman whose in-your-face approach showcased the power of impression. Margaret Louise was born to an outspoken, radical father who taught her to stand up for what she believes in and made sure she always spoke her mind.

Her mother, by age 50, after 18 pregnancies, 11 live births, and seven miscarriages, died from tuberculosis. Witnessing her mother's struggles cemented Margaret's decision to become a nurse and care for pregnant women. Her sisters supported her through college and by 21 she was able to start nursing training.

Ms. Higgins got married two years later and gave up her education. She gave birth to three children and was plagued by a recurring active tubercular condition. In 1911, when her house burned down, Sanger went back to nursing to help support the family. A year later, at 33 years old, she gave up her nursing career to work more deeply with her passions, women's health and sex education. During this period in her life, Margaret ran into her first episode of censorship by writing an article about venereal disease. This really set her in motion.

Sanger became even more determined than ever to fight for a woman's right to have proper information and control of her body. By age 35, Margaret was separated from her husband and enjoying the affections of several lovers. At around that time, she published her first issue of a magazine containing sex education for radical feminists, for which Margaret Louise was indicted on nine charges.

Her response was to flee to England in an attempt at avoiding the charges. While in England in 1915, at age 36, Sanger was arrested and sentenced to 30 days in jail for distributing sexual education material. In October, 1915, Margaret returned to the US to face the charges against her and gain media attention for her cause. One month later, her five-year-old daughter died suddenly of pneumonia.

Eventually, all charges against her were dropped, and Ms. Margaret embarked upon a world tour to promote birth control. As a first-hand witness to botched abortions, she gained a higher charge to invest a great deal of effort communicating with the general public.

A year later, at age 37, Sanger opened the first birth control clinic in the United States. Nine days later the police closed down the clinic. She and her staff were arrested, charged, and convicted to a 30 day jail sentence. She became the first women in the U.S. to be force fed in jail.

By 1921, her divorce with her 1st husband was final and Margaret married her 2nd husband in 1922. Ms. Sanger learned how to exploit a loophole in the political process to allow physicians to distribute health information to patients, establishing the first legal birth control clinic in the United States in 1923. Over the course of her career, Margaret was arrested at least eight times for expressing her views.

Throughout her life, she continued to be a force in the American reproductive rights movement and woman's rights movement. Mrs. Sanger died one year after the United States legalized birth control.

9

Access to Abortions

ICONIC
GAME-CHANGER
FOR FEMINISM

Norma Leah McCorvey possessed an ability to stand firm in her convictions, demonstrating how bold determination brings forth power. She was raised as a Jehovah's Witness. Her grandmother was a prostitute and fortuneteller. Her father was a television repairman; her mother an alcoholic. Norma had a difficult childhood, including being sexually assaulted by both a nun and a male relative along with dealing with her parents' divorce.

By age ten, she was declared a ward of the state after Norma stole money from a gas station to run away with another girl, she was later caught kissing. From 11 to 15 years old, she was in and out of state facilities for girls, dropping out of school at 14.

In 1963 Norma got a job at a restaurant where she met and married her first husband at 16. She left him when she was pregnant after he abused her. Norma moved in with her mother and gave birth to her first child. By 1965 she began to drink heavily and identified as a lesbian. Her mother tricked her into signing adoption papers and kicked her out the house.

What followed for Norma were years of bi-sexual activity, alcohol and drug abuse, and jobs that varied widely such as bartender and carnival barker. She had an affair with a co-worker resulting in a second pregnancy when she was 19. Norma gave the baby up for adoption. In 1969, at the age of 21, while working low-paying jobs and living with her father, she became pregnant a third time. Norma attempted to get an illegal abortion, but the clinics had been closed down. She was referred to attorneys who were seeking file a class-action lawsuit to change the abortion laws.

They were looking for a "Jane Roe" from pregnant women who were seeking an abortion. She fit the client profile the lawyers needed to represent for all women seeking abortions…young, poor, and white. Under the pseudonym Jane Roe, she met with the lawyers a second time to sign a legal affidavit she did not read. That would be the last time Norma would speak with the lawyers.

In 1970, when her case was filed in court, she was six months pregnant. A few months later, at 23, Norma gave birth to her third child and put it up for adoption. Two years later, she found out she had won her history-making case, Roe vs. Wade, from the newspaper, just like the rest of the nation. She wasn't called to testify or attend the trial. As Jane Roe, she had been a part of making history about abortions yet had never had an abortion herself.

For several years after, Norma and her lesbian lover would stay out of the spotlight and she would not become pregnant again. In 1992, she went on to work in abortion clinics, holding the hands of women and offering reassurance as they terminated their pregnancies, and making appearances on the Roe anniversaries.

In 1995, Norma met a seven-year-old girl who forever changed her life. The girl showed genuine interest, love, hugs, and invited her to church. Norma became convinced of the pro-life position, denounced her lesbian relationship, and converted to Christianity. She still maintains these views today.

VIII. Coochie Power in Sexuality

The lack of a public presence for individuals who assumed different genders began to change in the mid nineteenth century as a growing number of single people left their communities of origin to earn a living, gain greater freedom, or simply see the world. Able to take advantage of the anonymity afforded by new surroundings, the Transgender Society grew in the United States.

Migrants begin to have greater opportunities to fashion their own lives, which included engaging in same-sex relationships and presenting themselves as a gender different from the one assigned to them at birth. 2015 brought us the most famous woman in transgender history thus far, Catlin Jenner, formally Bruce Jenner. Catlin Jenner, two-time household name, has shattered the glass-understanding of many. Transgenderism has been taken to the next stratosphere. The LGBTQ communities represent living examples of the audacity to be who you are.

10

First Lesbian Organization

ICONIC
GAME-CHANGER
FOR FEMINISM

Dorothy Louise Taliaferro "Del" Martin and **Phyllis Ann Lyon's** bold willingness to be transparent about themselves projects how power can be obtained through daring actions. They are an American, lesbian couple whose fierce actions have helped shape the feminist movement and gay-rights activism, founding the first social and political organization for lesbians in the United States.

Del and Phyllis met in 1950, working as journalists at the same magazine. They became lovers in 1952 and moved in together in 1953. Two years later, they founded the first social and political organization for lesbians in the United States. For a decade, Del and Phyllis worked persuading ministers to accept homosexuals into churches. They used their influence to decriminalize homosexuality in the late 1960s and early 1970s.

Del and Phyllis became politically active in the first gay political organization, influencing a citywide bill to outlaw employment discrimination for gays and lesbians. In 2004 they were married in the first same-sex wedding in San Francisco, which was voided by the Supreme Court six months later. After being together over 50 years, Del and Phyllis legally married again four years later, in 2008, in the second first same-sex wedding to take place in San Francisco.

11

Documented Transgender Woman

ICONIC
GAME-CHANGER
FOR FEMINISM

Lucy Ann Lobdell's unapologetic rebellion to conform exuded the unbridled power of fearlessness. Born in 1829 to a working-class family, Lucy was never seen as your average girl. She was considered handsome, wore her brother's clothes, worked on the farm, in her father's saw mill, and was an expert marksman, giving her the nickname "The Female Hunter." Lucy left home for advanced schooling at 18 years old, having rejected a couple marriage proposals.

In 1851 Lucy married, giving in to his persistent four year courtship, and had a baby. Only to be deserted by him a year later. Lucy and her little baby moved back home with her parents, where she hunted and shot deer to provide for her family. In 1854, at age 25, Lucy changed her name to Joseph, authored her autobiography, got engaged to a woman and was chased out of town by people with tar and feathers.

Lucy left her parents and child behind, then deciding to permanently live as a man and earn a man's wages. In 1861, Lobdell moved into a Poor House, where she met a young woman from a wealthy family who was abandoned by her husband and too ashamed to tell her parents. The two became very close and when authorities refused to allow them to leave together, they ran away.

They wandered about the county for the next decade, living in caves, and eating roots, berries, and wild game. In 1871, Lobdell was arrested and jailed for impersonating a man, which over a decade, was followed by several run-ins with the law. In 1878, Lobdell's brother helped her claim money owed to her from her previous marriage. A year later the same brother filed a fake obituary to say she was dead and corroborated to have her committed to an asylum.

While in the asylum, Lobdell was diagnosed as transgender. She outlived all her family members who schemed to have her committed before dying in the asylum at age 83 in 1912.

IX. Coochie Power in Politics

At the beginning of the twentieth century, women were treated as outsiders to the formal structures of political life: voting, serving on juries, and holding elective office. They were subject to wide ranging discrimination that marked them as secondary citizens.

It is vivaciously electrifying to know that America, the land of the free, is on the verge of having its first woman as President of the United States. This would actualize the dreams of the past and ignite future generations of girls to dream.

12

Woman's Right To Vote

ICONIC
GAME-CHANGER
FOR FEMINISM

Susan B. Anthony's heroic commitment to the cause demonstrates the power of dedication. Born into a Quaker family committed to social equality, Susan developed a sense of justice and moral zeal early in her live. At age of 17, she collected anti-slavery petitions.

Susan also was sent to a boarding school where she unhappily endured its severe atmosphere. After one term, because her family was financially ruined, she got a job teaching. After teaching for fifteen years, Miss Anthony became active in the temperance movement. Since she was a woman, she was not allowed to speak at temperance rallies, which charged her to want change even more.

In 1851, Susan met a friend and acquaintance whose

meeting led her to join the women's rights movement in 1852. She spent a tremendous amount time with the pioneer of the movement. Soon after, Anthony completely dedicated her life to women's suffrage. The two women had complementary skills. Susan excelled at organizing, and the other had an aptitude for intellectual matters and writing. Together, they notably created some of the greatest strides for the women's rights and women's suffrage movements.

Ignoring opposition and abuse, Susan traveled, lectured, and canvassed across the nation for the vote. Ms. Anthony remained unmarried because she fiercely opposed laws that gave husbands complete control over the marriage. This gave her an important business advantage in this work. A married woman at that time could not freely sign contracts for convention halls, printed materials, and other documents. Susan also campaigned for the abolition of slavery, the right for women to own their own property and retain their earnings, and she advocated for women's labor organizations.

In 1900, Anthony persuaded a university to admit women by promising her life insurance. In 1872, at 52 years old, she was arrested and charged with illegally voting. Her trial was a major step in the transition of the women's rights movement into the women's suffrage movement. Susan Anthony never married. She was aggressive and compassionate by nature. She had a keen mind and a great ability to inspire and remained active until her death.

13

First Woman to Officially Run for US President

ICONIC
GAME-CHANGER
FOR FEMINISM

Victoria Claflin Woodhull's legacy packed authoritative, risk-taking power. Her life of unapologetic dedication to women's rights, free love, and anti-slavery was magnetic.

She was born in 1838 to a mother that was illiterate and illegitimate and a father who was a conman and snake, oil salesman. By age 11, Victoria had only three years of formal education. Her teachers found her to be extremely intelligent. She was forced to leave school because her dad committed insurance fraud by burning down his family's rotting mill.

Victoria was married three times, her first marriage at age 15. She had two children by her first husband, one of whom was disabled. Victoria found her first husband to be a womanizer and alcoholic and divorced him after about ten years of marriage.

At 27, Victoria married her second husband, who supported her ideals and introduced her to several reform movements. By age 32, she had gone from rags to riches twice. Woodhull and her sister became the first women to found a newspaper and open a business on Wall Street.

Victoria became most noted for being the first woman to run for President of the United States. She learned how to infiltrate the all-male domain of national politics and arranged to testify before the House Judiciary Committee, becoming the first woman to ever petition Congress in person.

It was even rumored that Victoria was a prostitute. She supported legalizing prostitution and free love. Ironically, Ms. Woodhull was jailed for publicly outing a member of the clergy for adultery, and her second marriage ended because of her adulterous relationship. She moved to England to get a fresh start shortly after, and was reported to be exhausted and depressed.

Victoria married her last husband in England at age 45. They did not often live together and they relied on corre-spondence to sustain their companionship. She remained a life-long activist for women's rights and labor reforms, also an advocate of free love, by which Victoria Woodhull meant the freedom to marry, divorce, and bear children without government interference.

14

African-American Woman to Officially Run for US President

Shirley Anita St. Hill Chisholm had an *Unbought and Unbossed* personality, which also happens to be the name of her autobiography, which demonstrated her ability to utilize revolutionary powers. She was born in 1924 to immigrant parents from the Caribbean. Shirley's father worked in a factory that made burlap bags and her mother was a seamstress and domestic worker.

Her parents wanted her to have a strong education and sent her to live with her grandmother from age 3 – 10. In 1939, Shirley attended a highly regarded, integrated, all-girls school. By 22 years old, she graduated from college where she earned a bachelor's degree, won prizes in debating, and joined a sorority. Miss St. Hill met her first husband that same year. They were married in 1949.

Shirley taught in a nursery school while going to school to get her master's degree in 1952. She became known as an authority on issues involving early education and child welfare. Mrs. Chisholm became interested in politics while running a day care and during this time she formed the basis of her political career. A court–ordered redistricting that affected her neighborhood convinced her to run for Congress.

In 1968, Shirley became the first African-American woman elected to Congress, representing her district for seven terms from 1969 to 1983. Ms. Chisholm's welcome in the House was not warm, due to her immediate outspokenness. Her seemingly dramatic decision to run for president came in part through her widely publicized opposition to the Vietnam-war. In 1972, Shirley became the first major-party African-american candidate for President of the United States and the first woman to run for the Democratic presidential nomination. Her first marriage ended in divorce in 1977. Later that year she remarried. Shirley had no children.

From 1977 to 1981, she was elected to a position in the House Democratic leadership. Throughout her tenure in Congress, Shirley Chisholm was a vocal opponent of the draft, supported spending increases for education, health care, and other social services, and reductions in military spending.

X. Coochie Power in the Military

During the Revolutionary War, women followed their husbands to war out of necessity. Many served in military camps as laundresses, cooks, and nurses, but only with permission from the commanding officers and only if they proved they were helpful.

Women have been a part of the war effort since the Revolutionary War, but in the early days of our nation they had to cloak themselves in disguise to serve alongside men. When they were accepted into the military, women were given auxiliary roles. As the weapons and methods of warfare changed in the late 20th century, however, the Pentagon began to realize that gender matters less on the battlefield.

15

First Woman Soldier

ICONIC
GAME-CHANGER
FOR FEMINISM

Deborah Samson Gannett possessed a courageous spirit that exuded how an adventurous spirit can be power. Born in 1760, Deborah was the oldest of seven children. When her father failed to return from a sea voyage, her mother, unable to provide for her children, placed them in various households. Gannett was raised by friends and relatives until she was ten years old, then she served as an indentured servant for the next eight years.

By the time she was 20, she had become a part time teacher and basket weaver. When Deborah first had the idea of enlisting in the army as a Continental soldier, since women were not allowed to be soldiers, she disguised herself as a man. Gannett was about five feet eight inches in height, which was tall for a woman. In 1782, she successfully enlisted in the army, under the name of her deceased brother, becoming the first American female soldier.

Deborah was almost discovered when she was altering her poorly fitting uniform and was observed to be very good with a needle. She fought her first battle and got cut across the left side of her head. Gannett refused to go to the hospital, fearing discovery, and tended the wound herself. Within weeks, she was hit in the thigh by a musket ball. She could not avoid being carried to the hospital. Once there, Deborah showed the surgeon the wound to her head, and he released her. She tried to dig the musket ball out of her thigh with her pen knife, without success. Deborah consequently had trouble with that leg for the rest of her life.

About a year later, she fell unconscious with a severe fever and was taken to the hospital, where the doctor discovered Gannett's secret. The doctor cooperated with her and concealed her secret. As Deborah was being nursed back to health, the Doctor's niece fell in love with her, thinking she was a man. Gannett had to confess and was honorably discharged in 1783. She had served for a year and a half.

In 1785, at 25 years old, Deborah got married a farmer and had three children. She later went on tour in 1802, capitalizing on her wartime fame, becoming America's first military female lecturer. In 1804, Gannett was awarded a pension by the State in the amount of $4.00 per month, because of her thigh wound. In 1818 it was doubled.

16

First African-American Woman Solider

Cathay Williams's androgynous ambiguity exuded the power hidden within gallantry. Cathay was born to a free man of color and a woman in slavery, making her legal status also that of a slave. During her adolescence, she worked as a house slave on a plantation. In 1861, at age 17, the war moved in and Williams was considered a captured slave and forced to serve in the military in a supportive role such as a cook, laundresses, or nurse.

By 1866, Cathay decided to enlist in the Army using her name inverted as William Cathay. She informed her recruiting officer that she was a 22-year-old cook. She was described as 5' 9", with black eyes, black hair, and black complexion. An Army surgeon examined her and determined the Williams was fit for duty, thus sealing her fate in history as the first documented black woman to enlist in the Army even though U.S. Army regulations forbade the enlistment of women.

Williams was assigned to the 38th U.S. Infantry and traveled throughout the West with her unit. During her service, Cathay contracted smallpox and was hospitalized at least five times, but no one discovered she was a female. After less than two years of service, it was discovered that she was a woman. In 1868, Williams was given a disability discharge but little is known of the exact medical reasons. By 1876, she had moved around a lot, been married to a man who ran off with her horses, and been a cook, laundress, seamstress, and also owned a boarding house. In 1891 Cathay applied for a disability pension based on her military service and was denied.

XI. Coochie Power in Finance

Throughout time women have exhibited an amazing financial fortitude. America's founding principals were designed to withhold women from the opportunity to exercise those abilities. Through much of U.S. history, women were dependent on others for their financial wellbeing. A woman's marital status had significant influence on her ability to control land, assets, or income. When women became more literate, received higher education including a better understanding of the legal restrictions that guarded their access to money, jobs, and land, they instituted change. Now, we have more opportunities to earn money, which is powerful because it gives us economic control and choice.

17

Married Woman Property Act

ICONIC
GAME-CHANGER
FOR FEMINISM

Betsy Love Allen was a woman whose defense of her birthright showcased how ancestry can be power. Betsy was born in 1780 to a highly influential, bi-cultural Chickasaw family who believed they needed education and owned slaves. Love married a white man at age 17 in a Chickasaw ceremony. She was his second wife and became the mother of eleven children. They all stayed with her parents, residing on her family's massive 100 acres of Chickasaw land.

In 1831, a lawyer sued Betsy's husband for $200 and ordered a sheriff to collect her husband's property for auction to take care of his debt. The sheriff seized a slave she'd willed to her child. Allen was around age 53 when she retained an attorney and sued for proprietorship of a slave she asserted was her lawful property before the marriage. Because Betsy Love Allen was an Indian and married under Chickasaw Tribal Law she was protected by treaty which says, any Chickasaw woman married to a white man had the right to dispose of her own property and the wife's property was not subject to the demands of her husband's creditors.

In 1837 Mrs. Allen won her Mississippi State Supreme Court case at age 57, which was followed two years later by the passage of the Mississippi Married Women's Property Act of 1839.

18

Black Commercial Enterprise Created Women Millionaires

ICONIC
GAME-CHANGER
FOR FEMINISM

Annie Malone's financial fortitude exuded entrepreneurial power. Annie was born in 1869 on a farm. She was the tenth of eleven children. Orphaned at a young age, she attended a public school before moving to live with an older sister. Annie attended high school and took a great interest in chemistry, but was forced to withdraw from classes because she was ill frequently. While out of school, she grew so fascinated with hair and hair care that she often practiced hairdressing with her sister.

Malone began to develop her own hair care products. By the beginning of the 1900s, around 30 years old, Annie was forced to move with older siblings. She experimented with hair and different hair care products, soon developing and manufacturing her own line of non-damaging hair straighteners, special oils, and hair-stimulant products for African American women. Malone sold her product door-to-door and began to revolutionize hair care methods for all African Americans.

In 1902, she moved to a thriving metropolitan city where she expanded her enterprise. Annie hired three assistants to sell her hair care products from door-to-door. As part of her marketing, she gave away free treatments to attract more customers. In 1903, around 35 years old, Ms. Annie briefly married, but soon divorced him when he tried to interfere in her growing business. The high demand for her product in 1904 led her to open her first brick and mortar location.

Malone also launched a wide advertising campaign in the black press, held news conferences, toured many southern states, and recruited many women whom she trained to sell her products. One of Annie's selling agents, who also became a millionaire, encouraged her to copyright her products to prevent fraudulent imitations and to discourage counterfeit versions. Six years later, Ms. Malone's business had grown so much she moved to a larger facility.

At 45 years old, she married a former teacher and bible salesman, and was worth well over a million dollars. That same year, she built a five-story multipurpose facility employing nearly 200 people. Annie's new facility housed a manufacturing plant, it contained facilities for a beauty college named after the product, a retail store where her products were sold, business offices, a 500-seat auditorium, dining, and meeting rooms, a roof garden, dormitory, gymnasium, bakery, and chapel. Her College's curriculum addressed the whole student. Students were coached on personal style for work which included coaching on walking, talking, and a style of dress designed to maintain a solid persona.

Annie Malone was able to create, through the school and franchise businesses, jobs for almost 75,000 women in America and globally. By the 1920s, she had become a multi-millionaire. In 1924, Malone paid the highest income tax in the state of nearly $40,000.00. She was extremely wealthy, but lived modestly, giving thousands of dollars to the local black community organizations, orphans, and colleges.

Annie's business thrived until 1927, when her husband filed for divorce. He demanded half of the business' value based on his claim that his contributions had been integral to its success. Over some time, she was able to settle for far less, $200,000.00. After the divorce, Malone relocated and bought an entire city block.

In 1937, at 68 years old and during the Great Depression, she was sued by a former employee claiming credit for her success. Annie had to raise money for the settlement by selling some of her property. Although much reduced in size, her business continued to thrive. At 88 years old, Ms. Annie Malone suffered a stroke and died. She had bequeathed her business and remaining fortune to her nieces and nephews; an estate valued at $100,000 due to her many losses.

XII. Coochie Power in Education

Over the past half-century, women have consistently dominated over men at school. In the early years of American history, women were discouraged from pursuing higher education. It was then considered unnatural for a woman to be educated. Women who advanced their education were considered deprived of sexual power. Over the last few centuries, women's positions and opportunities in the educational sphere have improved dramatically. Women now earn the majority of master's degrees and doctoral degrees in the U.S.

19

Women Getting Higher Education

ICONIC
GAME-CHANGER
FOR FEMINISM

Catherine Brewer Benson's birthright exuded the power of generational privilege. Catherine was born in 1822, the oldest daughter of parents who always planned to educate their children. They migrated south when her father got word of a possible opportunity for women to go to college. At 17, Catherine was shortly enrolled in a female seminary. The seminary closed around the time a new school for women opened.

Brewer, along with her father who was there for support, arrived to enroll on opening day. In 1839, she and nineteen other women from the seminary registered, attending the first female college. The very next year, Brewer and eleven other women became pioneers in education. Since her name was first alphabetically, she became one of the earliest women to earn a college bachelor's degree in the U.S. In 1842, Catherine got married at age twenty.

Over time, she had ten children and her interests were largely centered on her home and family. Mrs. Benson regularly attended alumnae meetings, which were organized in 1859, and the first association of its kind in the world. At 66 years old, she spoke to the graduating Class of 1888.

20

African-American Women Getting Higher Education

ICONIC
GAME-CHANGER
FOR FEMINISM

Lucy Ann Stanton possessed a passionate commitment which exuded fearless power. She was a testament to the many strong, resilient, and radical women that participated in the first-wave of American feminism. Lucy Ann was born free, the only child of her parents. When her biological father died, she was only 18 months old. Her mother married an abolitionist famous for his participation in the Underground Railroad.

Her step-father also believed in education. He started a school for free African American children, which she attended. Throughout Lucy's childhood, her step-father would harbor as many as 13 runaway slaves in their house at any given time. In 1846, at 15 years old, she enrolled in college. Four years later, Stanton graduated from college, becoming the First African American to complete a 4-year course of study at a college.

Straight out of school, she began working as a free school principal. Two years later, at 21 years old, Lucy Ann married her husband whom she met in college. She later began working as both a librarian and later an editor for one of the first abolitionist newspapers. In 1854, with a story in the same newspaper, Lucy Ann became the first African American published fiction writer.

She was 27 years old when she had a daughter in 1858 and the very next year her husband abandoned her, moving overseas. Stanton worked as a seamstress and continued her activism during the six years it took her to successfully receive a divorce in 1872. Her activism duties sent her to teach freed slaves in other states. While traveling, Lucy Ann met her second husband, whom she married in 1878 at 47 years old.

She and her husband later moved to Tennessee, where during the 1880's and 1890's, she continued to be a supporter of women's and African Americans' rights. Lucy Ann Stanton was an officer in the Women's Relief Corps, a grand matron of the Order of Eastern Star, and president of a local chapter of the Women's Christian Temperance Union. She died in Los Angeles at the age of 78.

XIII. Coochie Power Around the WORLD

21

Reigned Over & Expanded an Empire

ICONIC
GAME-CHANGER
FOR FEMINISM

Alexandrina Victoria was Queen, at 20, of the United Kingdom of Great Britain and Ireland from 837 until her death. It was a period of industrial, cultural, political, scientific, and military change within the United Kingdom, and was marked by a great expansion of the British Empire. Alexandrina's reign of 63 years and seven months is the longest of any other British monarch and the longest of any female monarch in history, also known as the Victorian era.

Moreover, should she remain in rule until Jan 2, 2017, her great-great granddaughter Elizabeth II will eclipse her reigning history.

Before Christ Historic Coochie Power

Hatshepsut was the fifth pharaoh of the eighteenth dynasty of Egypt. She came to the throne of Egypt in 1478 B.C., one of the first women to hold the rank of pharaoh. Hatshepsut took care of her people and built temples to the gods as well as other public buildings. Egyptian women in ancient Egypt were ahead of their time. They could not only rule the country, but also had many of the same basic human rights as men.

XIV. Coochie Power in the Youth

Malala Yousafzai was born on July 12, 1997, in Mingora, Pakistan. As a child, she became an advocate for girls' education, which resulted in the Taliban issuing a death threat against her. On October 9, 2012, a gunman shot Malala when she was traveling home from school. She survived, and has continued to speak out on the importance of education. She was nominated for a Nobel Peace Prize in 2013. In 2014, she was nominated again and won, becoming the youngest person to receive the Nobel Peace Prize.

Mo'ne Ikea Davis was born on June 24, 2001 in Philadelphia, Pennsylvania. She is an American Little League Baseball pitcher and was one of two girls who played in the 2014 Little League World Series. She is the first girl to earn a win and to pitch a shutout in Little League World Series history. She is the 18th girl overall to play, the sixth to get a hit, and the first African-American girl to play in the Little League World Series. She is also the first player to appear on the cover of Sports Illustrated as a Little League player.

Jazz Jennings was born October 6, 2000 in South Florida. She is an American transgender girl, YouTube personality, spokesmodel, and LGBTQ rights activist. She is notable for being one of the youngest publicly documented people to be identified as gender dysphoric and for being the youngest person to become a national transgender figure. She received national attention in 2007 when an interview with Barbara Walters aired on 20/20, which led to other high-profile interviews, appearances, and her own television show.

XV. Coochie Power in NOW

First Transgender Working at the White House

Raffi Freedman-Gurspan was born in1987 in Intibuca, Honduras. She was adopted while still an infant, and grew up in Massachusetts. She is an outreach and recruitment director at the White House. She is the first openly transgender staff member there and was the first openly transgender woman to work at the Massachusetts State House.

Potentially the First Woman as United States President

Hillary Clinton was born in 1947, in Chicago, Illinois. She served as first lady from 1993 to 2001, and then as a U.S. senator from 2001 to 2009. She unsuccessfully announced a bid for the presidency in 2007. Not to be discouraged, her faithfulness to serve led to her position as Secretary of State from 2009 until 2013. Spring of 2015, she announced her plans to fulfill her destiny and run again for the U.S. presidency.

First Black Woman Trillionaire Net Worth

Suzanne Shank was born in Savannah, Georgia. She started on Wall Street two days before Black Friday in1987, and subsequently was laid off. By 2014, she was the first black woman to head a publicly traded financial services institution when she was promoted to CEO of a Financial Corporation.

XVI. Future Coochie Power

Working to harness the courage of the women before us, better cooperation with each other, using our unique powers, and moving on to what happens next with absolute zest and zeal would be the ideal and ultimate outcome.

No-Judgement-Zone

Can you imagine having a completely judgement-free open dialogue? Not having to think about if you being politically correct? Wondering if you are saying the right thing? If you are going to make someone mad? There is so much to be learned from generation to generation. Opening the doors to share and taking the time to listen will begin to repair the broken bridges of the past, heal ancient wounds, and resurrect historical wisdom.

Keys to No-Judgement-Zone Conversations.

- Be open.
- Be real.
- Be patient.
- Be uncomfortable.
- Put good intentions out into the world and good intentions come back to you.

Our Bodies

I'm going to ask you to enter the No-Judgement-Zone with me. Most adult, grown, mature women call their private parts everything but what it is: a vagina. There are so many nicknames for our vaginas. I'm pretty sure, right now, you're thinking about your vagina's name. So let's get to the real deal. It's 2015. We have the Internet. If you have any type of relationship with someone born after Y2K, the year the Internet didn't die, they have access to this information.

We are metaphorically talking about repairing a broken bridge to a strong, secure structure that can sustain future growth. Some things may be better learned from the wisdom of a mature, grown, older adult, like how to love, honor, and respect the vagina and ourselves as women. So, if we are not acknowledging that we have a vagina, how can the next generation be taught to love, honor and respect their vagina? One woman's wisdom, honesty, and truth about her vagina helps to liberate another woman.

Passing Wisdom

Why take wisdom with you when you die when you can let it live through the next generation? Human evolution has brought us from the days of smoke signals, when passing wisdom ensured survival, into the days of mobile signals, where without a signal we feel unable to survive.

In the past, getting wisdom from an elder held special purposes like a rite of passage, entertainment, education, helping ensure future leadership, and survival skills. Now we

78

have Google, but Google cannot replace Grandma. It seems that what we used to know as Big Momma is dead and gone. The old-school Big Momma's dedicated their lives to taking care of the children, any and everybody's children.

Today's grandmothers are so different. They're social, active, and living their lives minus the muumuus. What will the fifth-wave grandma evolve into? Just like in the past, making time to share and pass wisdom is key to the next generation.

Personal Coochie Power

After reading this book, you can't help feel an incredible outpouring of respect and adoration for the spirit and power of the women's 21 game changing moves. Their personal and humanitarian quests provide deep and meaningful demonstrations of a **F.O.C.U.S. Mentality**.

Filter
Out
Circumstances
Undermining
Success

Unarguably, in order for the 21 moves to have taken place, a tremendous amount of FOCUS was demonstrated. It is extraordinary and fortunate for us to have their legacy as a guide to what is possible. That same spirit of wanting a better life for women as a whole, which was once alive in them, has been passed down and now resides in all of us.

The desire to have better and do better still resides in all of us. The time for better is right now, understanding that it's up to us to support each other and rally together.

Reader's Guide

1. Can you be empowered from the past?

2. What will you contribute in the future?

3. What wisdom do you have to share?

4. What topic(s) would you like to hear wisdom about?

5. Can you honor the No-Judgement-Zone?

6. When will you take a step to begin?

7. Will you leave this earth with wisdom someone needs?

8. Will you be open to sharing your wisdom?

9. Will you be open to absorbing wisdom?

10. What will your role be?

References

A Strange Story the Herald & Torch Light, Hagerstown, Maryland: September 13, 1871
Retrieved from: http://www.oneonta.edu/library/dailylife/family/lucy.html

"Amazing Life page". Sojourner Truth Institute site. Retrieved from:
http://www.sojournertruth.org/History/Biography/NY.htm

Barron, James (January 3, 2005). "Shirley Chisholm, 'Unbossed' Pioneer in Congress, Is
Dead at 80". The New York Times.

Biography.com Editors, "Margaret Sanger Biography." A&E Television Networks.
(September 21, 2015) Retrieved from: http://www.biography.com/people/margaret-sanger-
9471186

Biography.com Editors. "Abigail Adams Biography." October 18, 2015. A&E Television
Networks. Retrieved from: http://www.biography.com/people/abigail-adams-9175670

Biography.com Editors. "Victoria Woodhull Biography." October 18, 2015. Retrieved from:
http://www.biography.com/people/victoria-woodhull-9536447

Boyer, Paul (2004). Notable American Women: A Biographical Dictionary, Volume 5.
Harvard University Press. ISBN 9780674014886.

Bradford, Sarah (2012). Queen Elizabeth II: Her Life in Our Times. London: Penguin. ISBN
978-0-670-91911-6

Brandreth, Gyles. (2004). Philip and Elizabeth: Portrait of a Marriage. London: Century.
ISBN 0-7126-6103-4

Brenkus, John (August 18, 2014). "Sport Science: Mo'ne Davis". ESPN. Retrieved from:
http://espn.go.com/espnw/video/11352094/mone-davis

C. A. Farnham, The Education of the Southern Belle: Higher Education and Student
Socialization in the Antebellum South, NYU Press, 1994, ISBN 0-8147-2615-1.

Cochran, III, A. and Lawrence, Kansas. (June 2004). "Sexual Harassment and the Law: The
Mechelle Vinson Case." University Press of Kansas, 2004. ISBN 0-7006-1323-4.

Cochrane, Kira. (December 10, 2013) "The fourth wave of feminism: meet the rebel
women." The Guardian. Retrieved from:
http://www.theguardian.com/world/2013/dec/10/fourth-wave-feminism-rebel-women

Cohen, Nancy L. "How the Sexual Revolution Changed America Forever." February 5,
2012. Counterpoint Press.

Cohn, D'Vera, (February 13, 2013). "Love and Marriage." Pew Research Center.

Compton's Interactive Encyclopedia. (1994). "Women's History in America". Retrieved
from: http://www.wic.org/misc/history.htm

Cooper, Forrest Lamar (2011). Looking Back Mississippi: Towns and Places. University
Press of Mississippi. p. 23. ISBN 9781617031489.

Dan Woodman, Johanna Wyn (2015). Youth and Generation. Los Angeles, London, New
Delhi.Singapore, Washington DC: SAGE. p. 164. ISBN 978-1-4462-5904-7.

"Deborah Sampson. How She Served as a Soldier in the Revolution—Her Sex Unknown to
the Army." (PDF). New York Times. 1898-10-08. Retrieved October 5, 2016.

"Del Martin & Phyllis Lyon". The Lesbian, Gay, Bisexual and Transgender Religious Archives Network. (October 11, 2015). Retrieved from: http://www.lgbtran.org/Profile.aspx?ID=124

Ellis, Joseph J. First Family: Abigail and John Adams New York: Alfred A. Knopf, 2010.

Freeman, Jo (February 2005). "Shirley Chisholm's 1972 Presidential Campaign". University of Illinois at Chicago Women's History Project.

Freeman, Jo. "From Suffrage To Women's Liberation: Feminism In Twentieth Century America: A Feminist Perspective." Mayfield, 5th edition, 1995, pp. 509-28. Women.

Freyer, Tony. (2003). "Meritor Savings Bank v. Mechelle Vinson." Dictonary of American History. The Gale Group Inc.

Garner, Carla. "Sessions, Lucy Stanton Day (1831-1910)". BlackPast.org. Retrieved from: http://www.blackpast.org/aah/sessions-lucy-stanton-day-1831-1910

Garrow, David (1998). Liberty and Sexuality: The Right to Privacy and the making of Roe v. Wade. University of California Press. ISBN 0520213025

Gates JR., Henry Louis and Wolf, Julie. "Cathay Williams: She Pretended to Be a Man to Enlist as a Buffalo Soldier." March 2 2015. Retrieved from: http://www.theroot.com/articles/history/2015/03/cathay_williams_the_first_and_only_female_buffalo_soldier.html

Gelles, Edith B. Portia: The World of Abigail Adams. Bloomington: Indiana University Press, 1991.

Gordon, Rachel. (October 11, 2015). "Lesbian rights pioneer Del Martin dies at 87". San Francisco Chronicle. Retrieved from: http://www.sfgate.com/politics/article/Lesbian-rights-pioneer-Del-Martin-dies-at-87-3198048.php

Henry, Astrid (2004). Not My Mother's Sister: Generational Conflict and Third-Wave Feminism. Indiana University Press. ISBN 9780253111227.

History of Meeker County, Minnesota. Chapter: Wild Woman's History--The Slayer of Hundreds of Bears and Wild-Cats, pp. 98 - 111. AC Smith: 1877. Retrieved from: https://en.wikipedia.org/wiki/Del_Martin_and_Phyllis_Lyon

Hooks, b. (2007) Ain't I a Woman: Black Women and Feminism. Boston, MA: South End Press.

Hughes, Alan (January 23, 2014). "Meet the 1st Black Woman to Head a Publicly Traded Financial Institution". Black Enterprise.com.

Imbornoni, Ann-Marie, History of the American Women's Rights Movement, Infoplease 2000 http://www.infoplease.com/spot/womenstimeline1.html

Jaffe, Sarah. (Winter 2013). "Trickle-Down Feminism." Dissent Online Magazine. Retrieved from: https://www.dissentmagazine.org/article/trickle-down-feminism

Kathryn Cullen-DuPont (August 1, 2000). Encyclopedia of women's history in America. Infobase Publishing. ISBN 978-0-8160-4100-8.

Khan, B. Zorina (2005). The Democratization of Invention: Patents and Copyrights in American Economic Development, 1790-1920. Cambridge University Press. pp. 163, 166–8. Khan provides a table of the states and their enactment of statutes in these three categories.

Klaber, William. (June 18, 2013). "The Rebellion of Miss Lucy Ann Lobdell." The Rebellion of Miss Lucy Ann Lobdell. Greenleaf Book Group Press. ISBN-13: 978-1608325627.

Kuzmenka, S and Ryder S. "Legal Rape: The Marital Rape Exception." The John Marshall Law School, 1991. Retrieved from: http://library.jmls.edu/pdf/ir/lr/jmlr24/18_24JMarshallLRev393(1990-1991).pdf

Lear, Martha Weinman "The Second Feminist Wave" The New York Times Magazine, March 10, 1968

Lee, Carol, (August 18, 2015). "First Transgender White House Official, Raffi Freedman-Gurspan, Gets to Work." Wall Street Journal

Lobdell, Joseph Israel, (Dec 12, 2011). "A Strange Sort of Being": The Transgender Life of Lucy Ann 1829-1912.

Longman, Jeré (August 19, 2014). "Sports Illustrated and, Maybe in a Few Years, a Driver's License". The New York Times. Archived from the original on August 26, 2014. Retrieved from: http://www.nytimes.com/2014/08/20/sports/baseball/mone-davis-takes-little-league-world-series-stardom-in-stride.html?_r=1

M. and Wadia, K. (2013) 'The Gender of News and News of Gender: A Study of Sex, Politics, and Press Coverage of the 2010 British General Election', The International Journal of Press/Politics, 18.

Mann, Herman. The Female Review: Life of Deborah Sampson, the Female Soldier in the War of Revolution. New York: Arno Press, 1972.

"Married Women's Property Laws". American Women. Library of Congress. Retrieved February 3, 2013

Married Women's Property Acts in the United States. Retrieved from: https://en.wikipedia.org/wiki/Married_Women%27s_Property_Acts_in_the_United_States

Martin, C. and Valenti, V. (2012) New Feminist Solutions Volume 8. #FemFuture: Online Feminism. New York, NY: Bar- nard Center for Research on Women, Columbia University.

McCorvey, Norma (1994). I Am Roe. Harper Collins. p. 11. ISBN 0-06-017010-7.

Merrill, Marlene Deahl & Lawson, Ellen Nickenzie. (1978-1983). Oberlin College Archives.

National Center for Education Statistics. Digest of Education Statistics. Retrieved from: http://nces.ed.gov/programs/digest/d12/tables/dt12_310.asp

New York Times. (n.d.). "Deborah Sampson. How She Served as a Soldier in the Revolution—Her Sex Unknown to the Army." (PDF). New York Times 08-10-1898.

Nichols, James Michael (14 March 2015). "Jazz Jennings, Transgender Teen, Becomes Face Of Clean & Clear Campaign". The Huffington Post. Retrieved from: http://www.huffingtonpost.com/2015/03/14/jazz-jennings-clean-clear_n_6864236.html

Norton, Mary Beth 'Either Married or to be Married': Women's Legal Equality in Early America," in Carla Gardina Pestana and Sharon V. Salinger, eds., Inequality in Early America (University Press of New England, 1999), 25-45

O'Connor, Molly. "Mitch McConnell says more women graduate from college than men do." Politifact. July 18, 2014. Retrieved from: https://en.wikipedia.org/wiki/Female_education_in_the_United_States#References

Prager, Joshua (February 2013). "The Accidental Activist". Vanity Fair. Retrieved from: http://www.vanityfair.com/news/politics/2013/02/norma-mccorvey-roe-v-wade-abortion

ProCon Organization. (n.d.). "Prostitution: Historical Timeline." January 20, 2013. Retrieved from: http://prostitution.procon.org/view.timeline.php?timelineID=000028

Program of Wesleyan College Alumnae Association Annual Meeting, 2007

Prostitution: Historical Timeline". ProCon.org. Retrieved from: http://prostitution.procon.org/view.timeline.php?timelineID=000028

Psycology Today. (n.d.). "Marriage, a History: Long ago, love was a silly reason for a match. How marriage has changed over history." Retrieved from: https://www.psychologytoday.com/articles/200505/marriage-history

"Queen Hatshepsut". Phouka. Retrieved from: http://www.phouka.com/pharaoh/pharaoh/dynasties/dyn18/06hatshepsut.html

Rampton, Martha. October 23, 2014. "The Three Waves of Feminism." Retrieved from: http://www.pacificu.edu/about-us/news-events/three-waves-feminism

"Roe v. Wade". Free Online Law Dictionary. 2014. Retrieved from: http://legal-dictionary.thefreedictionary.com/Roe+v.+Wade

Schuster, J. (2013) 'Invisible feminists? Social media and young women's political participation', Political Science, 65.

Sessions, Lucy Stanton Day. (1831-1910). "The Black Past: Remembered and Reclaimed." Retrieved from: http://www.blackpast.org/aah/sessions-lucy-stanton-day-1831-1910

Shirley Chisholm, Unbought and Unbossed: Expanded 40th Anniversary Edition, Take Root Media, 2010.

Sojourner Truth Biography. "Children, Life Achievements & Timeline." Retrieved from: http://www.thefamouspeople.com/profiles/sojourner-truth-2873.php

Sojourner Truth Biography. Encyclopedia of World Biography. Retrieved from: http://www.notablebiographies.com/St-Tr/Truth-Sojourner.html

"Sojourner Truth page". Women in History site. Archived from the original on July 16, 2008. Retrieved from: https://web.archive.org/web/20080716114118/http://www.lkwdpl.org/wihohio/trut-soj.htm

Solidarity Organization. (n.d.). A Selective History of Marriage in the United States, "Timeline of civil marriage in the United States." 2015. Retrieved from: http://www.solidarity-us.org/node/370

Steindorff, George; Seele, Keith (1942). When Egypt Ruled the East. University of Chicago. p. 53.

Taylor, Jr., Stuart. "SEX HARASSMENT ON JOB IS ILLEGAL." June 20, 1986. Retrieved from: http://www.nytimes.com/1986/06/20/us/sex-harassment-on-job-is-illegal.html

The "ten or twelve" figure is from the section "Her brothers and sisters" in the Narrative (p. 10 in the 1998 Penguin Classics edition edited by Nell Irvin Painter); it is also used in Painter's biography, Sojourner Truth: A Life, A Symbol (Norton, 1996), p. 11; and in Carleton Mabee with Susan Mabee Newhouse's biography, Sojourner Truth: Slave, Prophet, Legend (New York University Press, 1993), p. 3.

"Transgender Teen Jazz Jennings Will Star in TLC TV Series 'I Am Jazz'". The Learning Channel. Retrieved from: http://www.tlc.com/tv-shows/i-am-jazz/

True, Jr. Phillip. Historical Personalities & Issues: QUEEN HATSHEPSUT (1500 B.C.). Retrieved from: http://www.nbufront.org/MastersMuseums/JHClarke/HistoricalPersonalities/hp3.html

Tucker, Philip Thomas (2002). Cathay Williams: From Slave to Female Buffalo Soldier (First ed.). Mechanicsburg, PA: Stackpole Books. ISBN 0-8117-0340-1.

U S History Organization, (n.d.). Women of Ancient Egypt, Ancient Civilizations Online Textbook. 2015. Retrieved from: http://www.ushistory.org/civ/3f.asp

U S Supreme Court. (n.d.). Meritor Savings Bank v. Vinson 477 U.S. 57 Court Case. (1986). Retrieved from https://supreme.justia.com/cases/federal/us/477/57/case.html

United States Army. (n.d.). Profiles of Bravery, "Cathay Williams" Retrieved from: http://www.army.mil/africanamericans/profiles/williams.html.

Weisberg, Jonathan (2004). "In Control of Her Own Destiny: Catherine G. Roraback and the Privacy Principle" (PDF). Yale University Press.

Wesleyan College. "Catherine Elizabeth Brewer Benson Class of 1840." Retrieved from: http://www.wesleyancollege.edu/profiles/Catherine-Elizabeth-Brewer-Benson-Class-of-1840.cfm

Whalin, W. Terry (1997). Sojourner Truth. Barbour Publishing, Inc. ISBN 978-1-59310-629-4.

Whitelocks, Sadie. (13 December 2012). 'I'm attracted to boys': Transgender teen who was born a male but identifies as a girl opens up about dating for the first time." Daily Mail. Retrieved from: http://www.dailymail.co.uk/femail/article-2247228/Jazz-Jennings-Transgender-teen-opens-dating-time.html#ixzz3oyyLSZ2b

Witchel, Alex. "Norma McCorvey; Of Roe, Dreams And Choices" The New York Times (July 28, 1994)

Woodman, Dan; Wyn, Johanna (2015). Youth and Generation Rethinking Change and Inequity in the Lives of Young People. London: Sage Publications Ltd. p. 122. ISBN 978-1-4462-5904-7.

Young, Alfred Fabian. Masquerade: The Life and Times of Deborah Sampson, Continental Soldier. New York: Alfred A. Knopf, 2004. ISBN 0-679-44165-4.

Young, Alfred Fabian. Masquerade: The Life and Times of Deborah Sampson, Continental Soldier. New York: Alfred A. Knopf, 2004. ISBN 0-679-44165-4 OCLC 52079888

www.ingramcontent.com/pod-product-compliance
Lightning Source LLC
Chambersburg PA
CBHW030028290326
41934CB00005B/530